HEART FAILURE

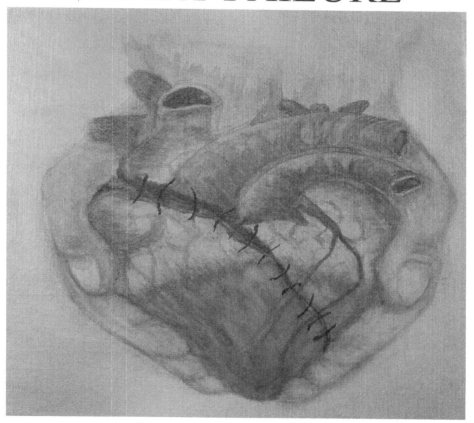

HEART FAILURE
Poetic Songs From A Broken Heart

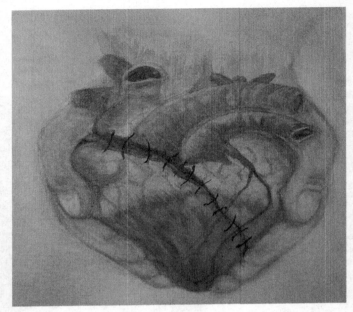

Mario Juliano Grande-Balletta

...dedicated to anyone who's lost at love, suffering from a broken heart, feeling regrets, haunted by a guilty conscience, seeking forgiveness & peace, tired of causing pain, and struggling to find themselves again...

TABLE OF CONTENTS

Introduction   Pages 7 - 8

Chapter One   -   "Julie"   Pages 9 - 17

Chapter Two   -   "Stephanie"   Pages 18 - 40

Chapter Three   -   "Ada"   Pages 41 - 56

Chapter Four   -   "Shirley"   Pages 57 – 59

Chapter Five   -   Random Poetry 2007 - 2021   Pages 60 – 73

Epilogue   Page 74

Conclusion   Pages 75 - 78

Bibliography   Page 79

Index   Page 81-82

Introduction

I never intended to publish my failures, or any of my poetry, least of all, what I wrote under emotional stress, sadness and depression. It always seemed too pathetic for sharing, too tragic and weak. I wouldn't have accepted the idea that anyone would want to read about my personal drama. Some very close friends convinced me to open the vault and share my vulnerabilities in public. So, several years later, here I am, revising and editing and publishing.

For most of my life, pen and paper rescued me from many forms of pain and suffering. I vividly remember withdrawing to secluded spaces, sometimes in hiding, to ponder over my saddest disappointments and find words to express my sorrow. It was my secret therapy as a child and has been ever since. I hid in closets, in vehicles, behind schoolyards, wherever there was solitude and peace. Many years later, I found myself writing in secret again, inspired by events that dramatically changed my life, and never expecting to share anything in public.

That was the case until recently. When I decided to title this collection of poems "Heart Failure", it was precisely because I realized how many times I had failed in love and relationships and caused heartbreak to others, with devastating effects and negative consequences, including to myself. I would retreat into my journals and notebooks to form poetic songs about my failures and personal tragedies and just pour out my feelings on paper.

This habit continued through most of my relationships. However, I only included poetry from the most pivotal, life-changing relationships in this volume. I had other relationships, besides the ones mentioned here, not too many, but some did not inspire me enough to record my feelings.

I tried to adapt this work to the typical publishing standards. The only exceptions are that I decided to include a brief history of each relationship ahead of the poetry and divide this volume into chapters. I wanted to describe the nature and background of each relationship and include an epilogue to summarize the final events..

I included this information to help the reader really grasp the sentiments, feelings, passion, sorrow, pain, suffering, and every other emotion I was experiencing during that time. I think it gives the poetry life and meaning.

In order to correlate this work to reality, I chose to present the poems and the relationships that inspired them in reverse order, starting with the most recent events in my life and then moving backward in time, from the present to the past.

Certain wounds are still fresh, despite the passing of time and the memories of certain events as vivid as the day in which they occurred. I hope you agree. I know the approach is different, but maybe you might find some inspiration or some comfort and recognize similar feelings in yourself and share with the world as I did.

Who knows?

CHAPTER ONE

"Julie"

I met Julie in Bogota, Colombia. We both worked for the same international technology company. I was assigned to work on an existing project underway in the Colombian office.

Julie was a programmer and had only been working for the company a short time, but she had already gained a respectable reputation for her diligence and aptitude, professionalism and courtesy. It was so evident that I too noticed her talent and abilities. Julie also captured my attention because of her serious personality, pensive demeanor, and intellect. I could sense she was very "real" and a "deep" thinker and not a superficial personality given to trends or popularity.

In other words, she was the personality type I wanted to attract someday and gravitated too! I was fortunate to have been seated directly behind her in the office and after a few days of only perfunctory pleasantries, we actually began to talk. In a short time, we learned about each other and our cultures. Each conversation was more intriguing and interesting than the one before and in a short time we could sense more than a friendship in the works.

The team of engineers and local staff would organize outings for lunch and dinner and sometimes included local music, dancing and drinks.

At first, neither Julie nor I participated, and we would hear about all the fun the next day. Then, after some gentle coaxing from colleagues, we both acquiesced and joined the group after hours.

What started as team building gatherings, soon evolved into drinks, music and native dancing. Our group would visit different establishments in the nicest parts of Bogota and we would dance till closing time. Julie and I always danced together and it became exclusive.

Once particular evening, I found a gigantic teddy bear in a department store and my instincts guided me and I surprised Julie with the teddy bear, almost larger than herself and she was ecstatic and surprised and very grateful. It was a pure gesture in innocence, regardless of my sentiments. I chose to remain stoic and chivalrous and not allow my feelings to develop into action on my part. I held my ground and believed she expected the same.

Time passed and the project ended, and Julie and I, never exchanged any expressions of affection other than holding hands from time to time and slow dancing.

I cried like a child on the flight home and was distraught and feeling a deep sense of loneliness and emptiness inside, wondering if she felt the same. We stayed in touch occasionally via email but essentially lost touch and Julie ended up leaving the company for another position.

I started writing down my thoughts about Julie during that flight home.

WHAT I SAW WHEN WE FIRST MET

I remember you sitting down, working from your chair,

something made my heart jump up and take notice,

I remember the innocent face and that long wavy hair,

I wanted to sit and talk and make sure i was closest,

~

who was this raven haired angel, exotic and subdued,

she spoke with wisdom and intellect beyond her years,

impressed by her thoughts and meanings and I pursued,

because i couldn't hold back despite my fears,

~

she amazed me and mesmerized with her gentle manner,

I felt safe and assured like I was with my family,

how could anyone be so happy and pure together,

this young woman was different, such an anomaly,

~

there were distractions hovering around us,

so many colleagues, customers and friends,

we got absorbed into this group consensus,

and danced away every night till the end,

~

what I really wanted was some special time,

time to learn how she became who she was,

with millions of questions waiting inside,

to discover her even more just because,

~

this young woman who became my Andean joy,

who gave me hope and so much inspiration,

a giant brute managed like a child's toy,

so eagerly trapped in loving admiration,

~

I was falling fast and every day it showed,

my desperate clinging and emotional attachment,

dreaming about marriage and a humble abode,

spending an eternity in utter contentment,

VIENDOTE

veo a las estrellas, y me brillan como tus ojos,

veo el sol y me calenta como tus abrazos,

veo a la luna y me encanta tu purez,

veo a el mar y noto la grandez de tu inteligencia,

~

veo a un jardin y gozo tus colores,

veo a una cuna y me siento seguro con tigo,

veo a las nublas y duermo feliz sonandote,

veo a el horizonte y me imagino nuestro futuro,

~

veo a un vino tinto y me recuerdo la nuestra sangre,

veo a una pareja anciana y pienso a la nuestra historia,

veo a los arboles y se cuanto hemos crecidos juntos,

veo a las nublas y me alegra una comodidad tan suave,

~

veo a tus fotos y me enamoro de la vida...

A COLD WINTER NIGHT

on a cold New England night,

I wonder where she stands,

to dream with all my might,

about beaches and silky sands,

~

she explores in Puerto Vallarta,

who knows what she is thinking,

I imagine her like any other,

whose beauty is just amazing,

~

seeing the world with just a glance,

her eyes pierce though any metal,

if life gives me one more chance,

to prove that my love is so special,

~

I melt when I see her picture,

I faint at the thought of her,

her image is becoming the fixture,

of my desires for our future,

~

a few thousand miles away,

the distance seems so far,

my love transcends the days,

it shines just like a star,

~

I hope she understands me,

does she realize my plight?

that a man loves so strongly,

on such a cold winter night...

TORMENTA DULCE

dulce huracan que rodea mi vida,

con vientos que llevan sabores desconocidos,

con poder y fuerza que me hizo girar de vuelta,

~

y a mirar el espejo de la vida,

que me saco de medio de una pesadilla triste,

y que me lleva a un paraiso,

~

en tu lado, siempre, tesoro mio...

LA VEDEVO

quando tramonto' il sole e' l'immagine sua splendente,

con l'aria del mattino il cielo ubicava l'orrizonte ,

~

mi riempiva i polmoni con la dolcezza sua,

morbida e sensuale perche, alla fine di tutto,

~

ti amo bella mia...

AFTERWARD

Years later, we reconnected via the internet again and our mutual respect, courtesy, chivalry and even some innocence seemed to return. We began to video conference and text and soon enough we were making plans to see each other after a decade had passed! It felt magical.

Julie and her mother and younger sister decided to come visit and we made definite plans and after visiting NYC for some time, they traveled north to visit with me and I was delighted! For 13 days I was in absolute heaven, and so appreciative of the company and genuine family style companionship. I felt reborn and alive again, like when love is brand new!

We shopped as a family, we dined, and we visited landmarks, places of interest, museums, and every night at home, we would relax and watch foreign films, sip teas and enjoy home made treats. The morning of my birthday, I awoke to balloons, decorations and warm smiles and gifts. I hadn't felt so loved and helpless like a small child at the same time since many many years. I was genuinely moved to tears.

Well, the time came for Julie and her family to return home and the last night, we talked about becoming official, identifying with each other as a couple, with the goals of marriage and of course, I was elated! I couldn't wait to announce it to the world!

That was the first time Julie ever kissed me and I will always remember that night.

The next day I was visibly distressed and shaken and emotionally saddened since I had to accompany everyone to the train station and say goodbye. The goodbye was very short, and almost distant, like the cold air outside.

We remained in contact for a while but Julie was not as convinced of our future as I was and her emphasis on more secular matters over shadowed my inclination towards matters of the heart and where communication failed, arguments arose and eventually, the dream died.

Apparently, I was much further along with my future visions than Julie was and once it became obvious I felt like a childish fool. We are still in contact today and a very large piece of my heart is still in Colombia, and with her family.

CHAPTER TWO

"Stephanie"

Stephanie was a beautiful, amazing, talented, educated, loving, and kind woman. She could easily assume the role of any magical princess or elegant queen, from any story or fairy-tale. Yet, she was remarkably humble, humanitarian in all her dealings and a natural born mother, a nurturer to one and all.

I met Stephanie as she was a waitress for a restaurant that would soon become my favorite, not only for amazing gourmet cuisine, but for wine and merriment and great times with friends and family. I always tried to schedule my visits when Stephanie was working. For some reason, I never could get the timing right.

Stephanie was engaged to her fiance and had been with him over 10 years. He was a musician. As my friends and I became regular visitors to the restaurant, we all began to establish a friendlier rapport and exchange superficial pleasantries among the occasional banter and always segue into life, music, politics, current events, social media, and many other topics.

We soon learned Stephanie was talented, attentive and captivating as well as aesthetically amazing, almost perfect from any angle, a pure delight to admire and engaging.

She was infectious to say the least and her eagerness to learn and grow as a person was inspiring and made us all appreciate life and the free gifts we enjoy in this world.

Time passed, and we always maintained a respectful, cordial relationship, and as often as I could afford, I would leave a generous gratuity since I knew she had many responsibilities and was struggling to support her household, pets, and even help her siblings. She is one the hardest most disciplined and focused workers you can imagine, just like any determined soul, she is a credit to her family and friends.

After my debacle with Ada had ended, I began spending more time at home and in between road trips, I would visit the restaurant to relax, enjoy the gourmet seafood and also to see Stephanie. As I became a regular with my friends, our conversations became more personal and at times, making inquiries about family, relationships, health, economics, aspirations, dreams, etc.

It was refreshing yet completely surprising to see such a beautiful young woman seemingly held back from greater pursuits due to economics and difficult relationships. Stephanie always maintained a respectful overtone when discussing personal life issues and her fiancé was no exception.

Despite learning about his many flaws and failures, we could admire her loyalty, patience, and devotion. It was attractive.

She certainly could have improved her station at any time and was not lacking in prospective suitors. We saw the deliberate attempts to ignore her privacy and relationship and how some would throw themselves in pursuit.

I did not vocalize my growing feelings toward Stephanie until the restaurant owners has confided to me in Italian that she was mistreated and not truly happy and could enjoy a much better life. It was hinted that I should remain a regular presence because her relationship would eventually end and she would be free.

The prospect of falling in love with such a gorgeous young woman was enticing indeed. So, I placed those ideas in the back of my mind. The attraction had begun and so had desire.

During one of my visits, I learned she had ended the relationship with her fiancé and she had returned to live at home. I was flying to West Africa for work and could not entertain any ideas at that time and weeks later I would send her my written plea.

While working in Ghana, September of 2008, I wrote a lengthy email and penned all of my personal feelings to Stephanie. I was terrified but I clicked and sent the email before I reason or logic could take hold and change my mind.

I didn't know how she would respond. She replied and said we would talk when I returned home.

Once I was home I visited the restaurant and learned all the details about her situation but was too afraid to ask her to associate with me, so we exchanged cell phone numbers and she asked me to join her at a bookstore some days later, it was our first official date.

I eventually met her family and a year or two later, she would meet mine. The beginning of our relationship was splendid, euphoric, mesmerizing, scintillating, and just amazing all the time. We fell in love fast and deep and an intense bond developed.

I had never dated such a beautiful woman, who genuinely loved only me, and she demonstrated her love in every possible way, more than I can describe, she was perfect. Stephanie inconvenienced herself to make our life together better, including moving furniture single handedly, handling secular matters, paying bills, maintaining contact with family and basically managing our lives like a dedicated team of over-achieving professionals.

Honestly, it was beyond comparison. Over time, as we moved from apartment to apartment, we reiterated our mutual plans to eventually marry and start a family. In the beginning I was so proud to imagine having a child with such an amazing soul mate.

Like the past, external influences, distractions and secular activities began to interfere with our bliss. I can only accept complete responsibility since it was my selfishness and neglect that allowed everything and everyone else to disturb our peace and bond.

Eventually, the decay would rot away any loving kindness and would mark the inglorious end of the greatest relationship. I filled my schedule with activities and appointments and gave away my time freely, without consideration for her needs. I became more neglectful.

Her love surrounded me 24 hours a day and everyone in my life realized how fortunate I was to have someone rescue me from myself and love like I had never been loved before and without conditions or reservations. All were amazed at the transformation she has given birth to in my life, through her constant efforts, validation, guidance, love, support and affection.

Stephanie was a domestic machine in the home rivaling any team of appliances. My entire life changed from disorder and chaos to order, including systems for filing, cataloguing personal effects, picture albums preserved for posterity, tools in their place. The difference was so noticeable that my productivity increased along with my desire to self-improve and thus, my self-esteem and self-worth reached new peaks!

As I basked in happiness I began to inherently take advantage of her hard work and love and selfishly spend my time in personal pursuits rather than reward the one who loved me so much and only wanted attention, affection and love in return. I was too busy and too occupied, yet I heard her pleas, listened to her emotions and still ignored her needs. I enjoyed being spoiled beyond imagination and returned very little in gratitude or affection.

I became complacent. I became distant. She warned me patiently so many times as my verses will show, and she begged me not to fail. She used to promise everyone she would not let me fail. She would make sure I would succeed this time. Little did she know, poor poor woman!

I will expound more details on my personal failures during the epilogue. Many of the poems will shed light on those failures and how I crushed and destroyed her heart and murdered love once again and condemned myself to guilt, pain and suffering.

Know that I truly loved her deeply with all of my heart. The poems that follow are full of sentiment that shows what I failed to communicate openly, but was very much alive in me, and happening inside, despite the silence. A restless heart knows no peace and I am proof.
I hope you can discern the love among these pages.

I will save the ending for the epilogue. Let's focus on what was positive and how the good aspects inspired the poetry that follows. The many verses that follow were inspired by Stephanie, by love and by music. The poems travel across the span of 7 years and end in heartache and tragedy.

Yet, I believe there is still a benefit in allowing others to see how open, alive, and raw the emotionally charged feelings were at the time. It is proof of how deeply seated love can entrench itself and how sadness and heartbreak can spiral downward into gloomy depression.
What follows is a perfect example of heart failure, in this painful context.

IN ONE YEAR

in one year the earth orbits the sun,

and in every increment of time I love her more,

~

in one year a website averages 300,000 visits,

and in every site I see her face and hear her name,

~

in one year 29,000 new songs are written,

and in every verse I hear three words,

~

in one year 136,000,000 babies are born,

and every one is innocent and pure like she is ,

~

in one year unlimited events transpire on this planet,

and during each one I loved her with my entire being,

~

in one year I will ask the question of a lifetime,

and in one year, I will have an answer!

ON MY KNEES

a shadow cast overhead as the grey looms forth,

a song of violins and horns to fill the cloudy morn,

the darkness recedes in fear of the solar light,

a reminder that day has come to remove the night,

~

I ponder my beautiful young friend both new and old,

in her quiet grace she reveals the hidden pain in her soul,

I seek answers from questions of a time no longer present,

to mend her wounds, dry her tears and give her treasures,

~

her sleep is troubled with thoughts weighed down like tons,

she dreams a world of tomorrow where nothing blocks the sun,

I see her gentle spirit fly and in the night it has cried to me,

calling me her friend and then i awaken gladly on my knees...

LOVE MAKES ME WONDER

I wonder if is there an end to my love,

does forever represent a place in time?

~

I wonder if i understand my own love,

can my emotional state become who i am?

~

I wonder if my love feels my mind,

can she appear in my dreams at will?

~I wonder if she knows i am writing now,

can she sense my thoughts tonight?

~

I only want to feel love all day long,

can i leave life and reality for love?

~

I need her touch to keep me alive,

can i draw her life force into me?

~

I love her more than my own life

I survive on our love every day...

UN DIA, UNA VIDA, Y UNA POESIA

imaginandote como te vi el ultimo dia,

recordandome tu cara de belleza,

~

y se que eres tu la luna y el sol de cada dia,

~

pensandote mujer, para estar con tigo siempre,

sabiendo que viviremos juntos nuestra vida,

~

y se que eres tu la duena de mi alma,

~escribiendote esta poesia me lleva alegria,

te la voy a leer con mi voz en persona,

~

y sabras que te amo cada dia, para toda mi vida,

con la dedica de esta poesia!

A BROKEN HEART

how do I mend a broken heart?

my entire world has fallen apart,

~

how do I find hope in a brand new day,

when the one I love has gone away?

~

my mind overflows with memories of you,

of all that we've shared, all that we knew,

~

I long for your touch and your warm embrace,

the look in your eyes, the smile on your face,

~

my dreams are filled with your soft gentle kiss,

I wake and cry for all that I miss,

~

how do I mend a broken heart,

when my one true love and I are apart?

~

my heart knows to love only you,

but it won't let go, so what do I do?

~

our moments together were precious and few,

but I cherished them all more than you knew,

~

I love you, my angel, and always will,

I loved you then and I love you still...

REGRETS

six years ago I wrote her a poem,

that poem was called in one year,

six years later without realizing,

I've hurt my loved one to tears,

~

six years of constant pain,

and never any relief in sight,

the emotional burden and strain,

replaced the once peaceful nights,

~

six years of stress and anxiety,

and never an ounce of gratitude,

I neglected her after my sobriety,

and I never seemed to improve,

~

I recklessly squandered all those chances,

meanwhile, she gave unconditional love,

I could have made such better choices,

but instead, I kept choosing for myself,

~

six year of guilt and so many sins,

she still forgave and loved me more,

in return I gave my time to my friends,

and forgot what true love is for,

~

six years to become an evil soul,

some dark distant emotional stranger,

guilty inside and full of voids,

living with shame and a giant empty hole,

~

now the world seems to be closing fast,

and there is no place to run and hide,

I regret my sins sprung this trap,

that has pushed her from my life,

~

here I drown in sorrow and useless pity,

every sad song is just another reminder,

how cold and dark this life really is,

without her love so warm and so tender,

~

I punish myself to fix our wounds,

how I wish I could turn back the clock,

and return six years to listen to the tunes,

that first made our hearts roll and rock,

~

our love was pure, strong and very real,

and I sang many love songs to her name,

I promised that in one year I would kneel,

and make her my wife and share my name,

~

as I face my newfound enemy, father time,

struggling to pour out a flood of emotion,

the danger of losing you in my life,

must be overcome by loving devotion,

~

I love you forever,

and I always have on the inside,

I strayed from guilt and personal dilemmas,

but this heart is still alive,

~

I miss you my only true soul mate,

and I know what I have done,

remember it's never too late,

for any true love to overcome...

HANGING AROUND LIFE AND THE PAST

lately I've been hanging my head in shame,

suffering for my mistakes from the past,

I lost the greatest love that ever came,

and graced my life for one last chance,

~

they say I should forgive and then forget,

and move on and start a new life again,

but all my thoughts and feelings never left,

and my heart is still in love till the end,

~

I hang around my world and no place to go,

realizing she was everything in my life,

no words or comfort can start to console,

the cold dark emptiness left deep inside,

~

I conjure up images and memories every day,

and try to remember all events and moments,

now she is no longer here and gone far away,

and the images fade fast and my heart laments,

~

I killed the one true love I ever felt,

and I murdered it slowly day by day,

with neglect, apathy and a love of self,

and let my guardian angel slip away,

~

she tried to help me many many times,

through reminders and songs and words,

she begged me to listen and she cried,

while I ignored the signs and went to work,

~

I focused on everything else in my life,

and I ignored the person who mattered most,

it doesn't matter how many times I cry,

she is gone and my heart feels the worst,

~

I will never be the same for what I did,

how I broke a beautiful young woman,

who loved me pure, innocent like a kid,

and I destroyed her heart and soul again,

~

I promised never to make her cry or hurt,

and for a while I was like prince charming,

my life got out of control and I did revert,

to baggage, emotional pain and suffering,

~

after realizing the greatest of all losses,

I finally sought the help I always needed,

I dealt with issues and my hidden demons,

I worked hard and then the layers receded,

~

I threw away all the guilt and shame,

and began to see myself in the mirror,

I no longer had any reason to blame,

and could see my life so much clearer,

~

many months later, as I finish this poem,

after weekly therapy and book after book,

I found Mario again and got to know him,

a man who stole her heart like a crook,

~

a man who loved music, arts and literature,

who also loved the entire world outside,

and could escape in spontaneous adventures,

thinking about the special woman of his life,

~

as emotions conjure up romantic gestures,

I dream of her beauty lying next to me,

my heart is healed and stronger than ever,

my eyes beg her presence so i can see,

~

Stephanie *******, story of my life

you are the only woman in my soul,

I pledge my existence to you, be my wife,

let's make our mark together in this world..

HIDDEN TEARS

it seems like a long long time ago,

so many memories finally coming back,

my mind travels this depressing road,

and my heart is under constant attack,

~

I hear a cascading waterfall of tears,

rushing downward from the inside out,

in absolute silence the past reappears,

and scripted scenarios play turnabout,

imagining somehow if things had changed,

through different words and expressions,

hoping to appease her drama softened face,

that longed for truth and loving validation,

~

wondering if she ever stops to think,

does my name ever appear in her mind,

are there any good times still linked,

or does her heart only punish crimes?

~

is she ashamed of ever loving me at all?

am I nothing more than a history of regrets,

my feelings are splattered on every wall,

extinguished like her Camel cigarettes,

~

its like reading an old favorite book,

and replaying memories like movie scenes,

time erases the details like some crook,

and I'm lost searching for the in-betweens,

~

I'm sure I'm not even a thought anymore,

and have been deleted from her life,

yet sad songs became the musical score,

reminding me she was going to be my wife,

~

how do I even measure how great a loss,

and does anyone even care to understand,

she really was the greatest love of all,

and now my heart is empty in the end,

~

move on everyone says and forget the past,

why is it so hard and impossible to do,

more than guilt and love hold me back,

and prevent me from ever shining through,

~

I have no pictures, cards or keepsakes,

in anger I destroyed everything in sight,

losing her was more than I could take,

my mind stored things like a hard drive,

~

the time has passed and she is married,

I'm older and the pain shows the years,

all this time her memories I carried,

and every night they calmed my fears,

~

I believe I must forget her now,

and it hurts to accept that fate,

she chose life with him somehow,

and my name must be full of hate,

~

why don't we listen when they cry,

why dont' we love back when they beg,

why do we ignore and just let things die,

and then we suffer so much in the end...

AFTERWARD

At the time the relationship ended, I descended into a state of shock, panic and intense heartbreak with all of the painful consequences. Despite my epic failures in matters of the heart, I still believed I would find the right time and place and turn things around and return us to the wonderful love we both enjoyed and thrived upon in the beginning. I was wrong.

People therapy taught me some important lessons I will never forget. No matter how much we change, improve, and monitor our own behavior and learn the value and pleasure of being unselfish and returning unconditional love to others, life does not guarantee any opportunities to repair the damage we have done in the past.

We may desire to express ourselves differently, with our newly adopted changes and want to demonstrate our progress, especially to the ones we hurt badly and love them again, however, it is selfish to intrude into the personal space of others who are no longer in the same relationship anymore, for they have moved on, found new love, and may not wish to be reminded of any failures, pain or sad memories from the past.

Until you forgive yourself, no one else can either and changes cannot become permanent until you accept responsibility for the past, accept the painful consequences, accept the corrections, accept the changes and then finally, accept yourself again, as a new person.

I had to learn those lessons the hard way, as usual, but I learned. My personal suffering was my tutor, each disappointment taught me tolerance and forgiveness, and each setback taught me patience.

I realize I lost the greatest love of all, precious, unique, beautiful, unconditional, altruistic, and completely devoted in loyalty. I neglected it and damaged it and injured it until it began to decay and rot and eventually it died, leaving behind many wounds and scars, some never healed, and a long trail of tears, enough to fill barrels.

Needless to say, as is only humanly possible, I said and did everything wrong and sealed my own miserable fate. My actions would eventually become my judge, jury!
I will never forget the lessons for the rest of my life.

CHAPTER THREE

"Ada"

I don't know how to prepare anyone for the details surrounding this relationship. It's not easy or comfortable. In fact, you may find the entire account repulsive, despite the veracity. This was a controversial relationship, to say the least. It started innocently enough, but quietly escalated until many sides of my extended family were embroiled in the drama.

Ada and I had not seen one another since the early 1980's.

After a failed marriage and tragic death of my daughter, I sought temporary comfort and distraction by visiting family in southern Italy.

I have a large extended family and had not seen many cousins in decades. The small reunions and get-togethers were like therapy and very instrumental in coping with personal tragedies.

When I saw Ada, and her sister, cousins and friends, I was amazed that who I knew as children were now adults, with experiences and a history of their own. I know what you're thinking, that is a bit naive, but given the circumstances and state of mind, understandable.

We began associating as a group, taking evening excursions to beach towns and cities and touring the countryside and visiting the ruins and relics.

What began as innocent tour guiding ended up as a torrid, intense, dependent relationship. It started one night at the beach, at Baia Domizia.

We had gone out alone without the entourage and had been doing so for a while, talking, sharing experiences of each other's relationships, life, etc. We explored our personalities and answered many questions, including difficult personal ones. We were bonding.

That night, we held hands and kissed for the first time. It was magical and despite flying home the next day, I knew I had changed and so had Ada. We had crossed a line but the taboo effect was so powerful, so mesmerizing and addicting, neither of us could stop.

Sure, she voiced the typical arguments and yet continued to call, write and text and join me for every rendezvous whenever I could visit, which was 5-6 times a year for several years.
Our secret rendezvous and European sojourns provided the scenery and backdrop for a very intense and romantic love story.

However, our mutual relatives were not yet privy to the details and were only accustomed to my family visits and our close association and daily excursions hidden from sight. We became inseparable, so much so that Francesca her older sister called us "due goccie d'acqua" namely, two drops of water, and we were obviously in the same bucket.

The poetry that follows was based on that same aspect of our relationship, our bond by blood, and our bond by love, my "secret weapon" a term I used often to affectionately tease Ada. I would learn than a weapon can be turned and pointed in any direction.

As is true with all romantic fables, good things come to an end. We all know matters of the heart are serious and intense and this relationship was no exception.

Once our feelings mutually intensified and we could no longer suffer distance, we began discussing our future, including relocation and marriage. Those sentiments are echoed in the verses that followed this account. I hope you will understand the circumstances.

DUE GOCCIE D'ACQUA

sono andato al mare,
il sole stava tramontando,
mi avvicinai verso le onde,
poi fu dalle goccie indossato,

~

pensavo sempre alla mia ada,
e le sue guancie di calore,
che ci fosse lei al mio lato,
bagnata con le stesse goccie calde,

~

vedo passare le onde,
ed il vento muove i tuoi capelli,
e mi sembrano foglie di passione,
brillanti e posati sui tuoi coralli,

~

le labbra del tuo sorriso,
bagnano l'aria del mare,
con il tuo corrente caldo,
morbido, dolce e sensuale,

~

la luna di mare mi coccola,
sotto la luce di mille candele,
pensando alla nostra storia,
e la nostalgia sempre bella,

~

nell'acqua si vede tutto,
perche chiarisce la realta,
e noi due siamo come le goccie,
lacrime d'amore per un' eternita

MARIPOSA DELICADA

la voz de mi querida me levanta
comos los alitos de una mariposa

~

me despierta con sus palabras dulces
y me llena la alma con sentidos amables

~

me hizo volar como un pajaro viajante
con el amor especial de mi querida volante

~

estoy tan enamorado de ella que por seguro
viviendo una vida sin ella sera muy duro

~

o ada prima mia, eres el aire que suspiro
llevandome a las alturas del cielo nativo

~

te pienso en ti durante cada segundo
recordandome que soy tan suertudo

~de conocer a una diosa verdadera
que vuela como la mariposa delicada

~

vuela y sigue volando mariposa especial
delicada y divina siempre con tu libertad

~

quizas la Ada, adonde se va a quedar,
seguramente ha escogido su proximo lugar

~

moviendose con Lorenzo, su bebe protegido,
que enfante inocente, puro y distinguido

~

la fin de mi vida dura miserable se ha presentado
que tantas tragedias y pecados me han castigado

~

animal, odioso desaparecido, miserable que soy
me deben olvidar y rechazar, toda la gente de hoy

~

Ada ******, pariente mia, tantas veces me amaste,
ahora de nuestra historia y mi amor te cansaste,

~

no se como sentirme mas, y quiero tanto a llorar
por que pierdo la unica persona que puedo amar

~

espana mia, mi esperanza, tierra madre colonial
con ansiedad me sueno de ser tu residente oficial

NEI GIORNI DI TE!

Nei giorni da dimenticare....

~

Ho messo in pericolo tutto cio che amavo
Ho rischiato con la cosa piu preziosa
Ho visto quasi crollare i miei sogni

~

Nei giorni dal buio....

~

Sono stato senza di te
Sono stato solo con la mia coscienza
Sono stato abbandonato con la tristezza

~

Nei giorni da riflettere....

~

Ho riconosciuto i miei errori
Ho incontrato allo specchio i miei difetti
Ho sofferto con le mie ferite

~

Nei giorni di silenzio....

~

Ho accetato le consequenze
Ho visto nascere le tue parole
Ho riconosciuto i tuoi pensieri

~

Nei giorni da pensare....

~

Mi hai risuscitato col tuo amore
Mi hai perdonato con la tua misericordia
Mi hai salvato con la tua umanita

~

Nei giorni da ricordare....

~

Ho sentito ancora il tuo calore
Ho tremmato quando mi toccavi
Ho pianto lacrime di gioia per te

~

Nei giorni della lontanaza....

~

Ti penso ogni secondo
Ti sogno tutte le notti
Ti vedo quando chiudo gl'occhi

~

Oggi, in questo giorno....

~

Ti amo con tutta l'esistenza mia
Ti accetto completamente come sei
Ti voglio con me per tutta la vita

NERO SUL BIANCO

nero sul bianco,
qui, sulle pagine ti scrivo,
con i segni sulla carta,
l'inchiostro, scorre cosi libero,

~

poi un verde sull'obscuro,
e nel buio si sente la schiuma,
come le onde del mare,
che di sera temono la verita,

~

onde e verita come vita e morte,
non si possono fermare mai,
come il tempo che sempre vola,
e la storia nostra che tu hai,

~

la storia del cuore,
che ci spinge verso noi,
due anime diventate una,
un amore cosi grande e' poi,

~

sono convinto e sicuro,
come la penna che scrive,
che sei il mio futuro,
affinche posso vivere,

~

un'anima vestita da pennino,
scrive parole dettate,
poi da un cuore solitario,
sono ripetute dall'eco

~

i cieli e le stelle non mi rispondono,
quando grito ti amo sempre di piu,
ma lei mi sente anche da lontano,
perche dentro di me, ci sei sempre tu!

LABBRA TUE

Ho letto le tue labbra con un bacio,
c'era scritto l'amore che mi dai.

~

Parole scolpite dal vento
sulla sabbia decorata di conchiglie.

~

Ho visto parlare il tuo cuore,
con le mie lettere d'amore.

~

Ho trovato scritto poesie
che parlavano dei tuoi sentimenti.

~

Labbra tremolanti e profumate,
calde e piccanti,

~

in sordina scrivevano
i nostri attimi felici,

~

i baci silenziosi,
i momenti d'ansia e d'intensa gioia.

~

Ho letto sulle tue labbra
la voglia di gritare felicità,

~di bruciare l'odio del mondo,
denunciare tutte le atrocità.

~

In quelli scritti,
c'era il desiderio di restare soli,
con l'amore e la passione.

~

Il mio bacio ha letto le tue labbra,
ed ha lasciato scritto ancora
le parole "amore per sempre".

~

Ho letto le tue labbra amore mio,
mille bolle di sapone dovrebbero innalzarsi

~

per contenere l'amore che ogni
tua parola sa donare...

LEI, L'AMORE E' LA PENNA

non c'e' l'istante in cui non ho voglia d'amarti,
l'ho sempre desiderato anche prima di conoscerti,
poi quando t'ho incontrata, mi sono innamorato appena visto,

~

stasera chiedero a questa penna di portarti,
viva tra le braccia solo un poco per sentirti,
poi la chiedero di darmi l'emozione tra le dita,

~

stretta come se stringessi te nelle braccia,
a sentire il calore della tua pelle con la mia,
senza guardare il tempo ne responsabilita,

~

cosi i miei pensieri volano come la penna mia,
che balla lasciando segreti su questi fogli,
che diventassero ricordi di una dolce storia,

~

lei e la ispirazione di me e della penna,
senza di lei non serviamo pui a nulla,
pensando lei nascono i sogni tra realta,

~

~quando inizio non so mai che devo scrivere,
sento la voglia di esprimere il mio amore,
con l'aria sole vento e le onde del mare,

~

in bianco e nero chiedo il suo cuore,
come penna e carta a me legati sempre,
la storia che viviamo e quella da scrivere,

E POI (2021)

stamattina, gl'incubi d'ieri sera mi hanno svegliato...
e poi, dopo una pausa, si riprese il mio fiato...

~

rimango bloccato per ore sane, senza capire nulla...
e poi, quando penso a te, parole diventano la folla...

~

emozioni mi circondano come stranieri al mercato...
e poi, incomincia il nuovo giorno e devo accetarlo...

~

nel sogno vivono pensieri nelle fantasie magiche...
e poi, lo sveglio ci ritorna alla vita primordiale...

~

lavoro e servizi, opere in casa, tutto normale...
e poi, mi ricordo che amo te, con questo cuore banale...

SEMPRE DI PIU (2021)

versano il formaggio sulla pasta,
ma io, sempre di piu

~

inviano migliaia di messaggi,
ma io, sempre di piu

~

sognano l'amore delle canzoni
ma io, sempre di piu

~

e si perdono dentro le follie,
ma io, sempre di piu

~

mangiano tutto quello che fa male,
ma io, sempre di piu

~

e poi sbagliano senza riconoscere,
ma io, sempre di piu

~

e amano senza condizioni,
ma io, sempre di piu

~

gli vengono pensieri inutili,
ma io, sempre di piu

~

e sono tutti incompatibili,
ma io, sempre di piu

~

e poi ci si ama per eternita,
ma io, sempre di piu

~

in ogni cosa di questa vita,
eccomi, sempre di piu

AFTERWARD

In time, as work, travel, time and distance began to take their toll, Ada and I had discussed

making our lives permanent, in Barcelona, Spain. We knew we would live in the United States

for a short while, but eventually, move to Spain. In addition, we were eventually discovered by

family and as expected, the interference began, along with the drama, meddling and external

influences. This added a stressful element in our lives.

We began exploring, making arrangements, and naturally, the greater family began to notice and

suspicions aroused about the nature of our "closeness" were finally confirmed when Ada's

pregnancy was discovered. A wedding was quickly planned, inviting only family, and some

relatives declined to participate which was unfortunate but their wishes were respected.

Near the time of the wedding, my mother, my true soul mate from this wretched human life, my

real sanctuary in this world, my confidant and tutor and greatest influence in my life, finally

succumbed to all of her diabetic complications and passed. I was devastated and suicidal.

For a short period, I was silent and focusing on work while time passed. Ada's family insisted we change the wedding dates and marry 30 days after the funeral and burial. I agreed.

Invitations were mailed, and a cathedral by the water was confirmed along with a fancy seaside restaurant for the reception. The honeymoon was planned for Barcelona too.

As the date arrived, I was traveling through the UK and Ireland. I was in Dublin and preparing to fly in for the wedding. As I paced nervously in the airport, my cell phone began to ring feverishly and relatives were calling from Argentina, United States and Italy.

I assumed most of the calls were festive and congratulatory in nature. Once again, I was wrong. Some relatives were happy for us and some were shocked. I tried to diplomatically summarize the circumstances and assuage any concerns.

As I engaged in multiple conversations with relatives, discussing our future and our plans, I noticed certain relatives started voicing concerns and issues about our nuptials. I was surprised and as I listened more and more, a dark cloud of uncertainty and doubt was forming. Once you add gossip and rumors of infidelity, emotional disaster loomed and and I felt the walls closing in fast.

As certain relatives swore oaths of secrecy to the highest authorities, I began to sink into a depression and fearful state and I pulled the plug on the wedding.

I didn't board the flight and instead changed my ticket and returned to Boston. I called Ada and explained what I had heard and that I needed clarification, truth and confirmation before entering marriage.

After a tragic marriage and many losses, I just couldn't afford the risks, not at my age. So, in a very short time, everything deteriorated amidst the rumors and controversy, a fairy-tale romance was lost, and the once ironclad bond between us was slowly severed and replaced with a fading platonic facsimile of relations.

The "authorship" of the pregnancy was now covered in a hazy cloud of accusations, doubt and suspicious circumstances. Once the relations ended, so did ties with Ada's family. Years passed without any contact. Connections disappeared from social media too.

Coincidentally, another child was born in Capua, on April 02, 2008. I will always remember that fact.

Later in the spring of that year, I visited family again with a close personal friend of mine from the gym. Ada greed to meet and she brought Lorenzo who was solid, strong, and quite loud. We met for lunch and espresso and Lorenzo could not be silenced. I intervened and took hold of Lorenzo who was instantly quieted which drew immediate anger and condemnation. I found it humorous, amusing and I was in complete delight that Lorenzo was comforted by me, a complete stranger, who's only connection was by blood. That was May 2008.

My poem's about Ada and I were written in Italian and Spanish. Unfortunately, my usage of Italian and Spanish is elementary at best and does not do these amazing colorful languages the justice they deserve.

I am sure any other talented write with a true command of would have really extracted much more sentiment and emotion from the words than I was able to do, therefore I apologize in advance.

It is obvious Ada and I were not able to wed and spend our lives in marital bliss, quite the contrary. For a time, we did maintain civil communications and the slowly drifted from focus. I understand she did participate in two other relationships since then and has since moved forward with her life and her child. I understand she has moved back home living with her parents. I often wonder if time and circumstances will allow us to meet again.

UPDATE:

I included two recent poems written for Ada during 2021.

CHAPTER FOUR

"Shirley"

Shirley was a teenage love of mine, the only one that I can honestly remember with passion and fondness sharing similar circumstances. She moved into my neighborhood suddenly and we instantly became two peas in a pod, despite my shyness.

She was a raven-haired, advanced curves and anatomy and street smarts sharp enough to cut through steel. But, she was also kind and loving and gentle when showing her vulnerable side. I will never forget her face and the way she made me feel as the first girl I ever kissed.

I left high school and joined the military and never saw Shirley again for many years. She had married and started a family and moved on and seemed very happy.

Decades later she has a wonderful family, amazing adult children and she is attached to her pets.

TWO TEENS

1986

two teens arrived from different roads

she traveled a tragic path and sad as she struggled

his road was dysfunctional and shaming and troubled

from another life they bore heavy loads

two wounded hearts crying rivers of pain

nightmares of broken trust and ultimate betrayals

a life of setbacks, disappointments and epic fails

souls in distress under clouds of rain

~

he didn't know the meaning of love

her world was changing from just one look

his heart was barren like an empty book

she prayed to someone up above

~

like a romantic movie the two became one

he worshipped her by day and in his dreams

she silently cried for him and her soul would scream

no two lovers would ever have so much fun

~

together like every song on the radio

they both swore to never be torn apart

a love so strong it would fix a broken heart

and then life changed and it was time to go

~

an evil stranger with a wandering eye

two young kids and a love so pure and fresh

a jealous predator lusting for her glowing flesh

a dream shattered by a treacherous lie

~

he ran far away into the darkness

she was left alone holding the bag

a beautiful love torn like a rag

a lonely heart tangled into a mess

~

decades passed and not a sight or sound

two lives lived apart on separate roads

two stories and events dying to be told

years later he finally came back around

~

this time she desperately needs to go away

and there is no evil stranger behind it all

there are only reasons and then freedom's call

once again the greatest love has gone astray...

CHAPTER FIVE

Unaffiliated/Random Poetry From 2007 – 2021

August 18, 2008 - Cranston, Rhode Island, USA

THE STORM IS MY SOUL

the sounds of thunder rumble beneath me and rattle my soul...

the cracking of nature's whip and stinging drops from the sky...

~

my face is drenched from the grey, wet darkness as tears roll...

i close my eyes, and my breathing slows, to where i lie...

~

the beating of the drops become the fainted rhythm i hear...

as my heart slows down, i feel something carrying me away...

~

a calmness overtakes me, and the presence of someone is near...

the fear is gone, and i need this presence to stay...

~

the sounds tranquilize me into a hazy slumber...

and the presence soothes me into a euphoric state...

~

i realize i am dying and will be passing over...

with the storm that absorbed my soul today...

September 25, 2008 – Aix-En-Provence, France

THE SUMMER WIND

the flower sways to and fro amidst the gentle summer breeze

the birds and butterflies dance nearby with a graceful ease

~

a petal releases pollen like sustenance to the air

a bumblebee, beckoned by sweet aromas to rest upon this lair

~

a child runs nearby with laughter brimming in delight

the sky's white cotton clouds will soon turn into night

~

again the wind hastens by with a gentle force

reminding all that the season takes its course

~

i felt the summer wind pass through my soul today

like a dream my life was changed forever in this way

~

i tell you cherish your summers and worship the sun

life years moves so quickly and then all is done

THE SANCTUARY

a darkened room, a cold floor and a quiet corner...

iIclose the door and retreat to this silent abyss...

eyes full of tears, a dampened face as my thoughts wander...

I sit and find the melancholy I always miss...

~

my pain is real, I feel the sting and hurt inside...

the weight is heavy and exhausts my strength...

suffering has become the mantra in this so called life...

it cannot be measured and is beyond any length...

~

a secret location to isolate myself with sorrow...

a private place for my soul to bleed

a shivering cold and wind which makes me wallow

a languid depression to come fill my need

~

I dream of a gentle death that waits for me

in my sleep it comes and draws me near

the time has come to depart my sanctuary

and leave this world no longer in fear...

September 24, 2008 – Paris & Marseilles, France

FRENCH RAIN

the sounds are muffled by the silent engines of the TGV

I gaze outside and see green fields dampened and cold

the sun has not given light to the Gallic countryside

~

many farms and villages are swept away at high speed

and the land is quiet this morning since the rain is bold

the roads are long and abandoned and not one person in sight

~

the accents from the french passengers are now my delight

I am back again to work and live with a goie d'vivre

I recoginize the towns and names of places I have seen

~

the next bottle of Gigondas will taste so much better

because today I have returned amid the french rain

I wait for Aix-En-Provence and then I will sleep

THAT PLACE

all of my emotionally cognizant life I have been aware of a place,

I have escaped to that place daily to find my pain and freshen my wounds,

~

the melancholy sounds of my music fly me away to that place,

I see grey images in another scenario, appearing as a living daydream with sounds,

~

action, people and scenes of my last hours on this earth,

I die a thousand times and the pain lingers in the present conscious mind,

~

I abandon myself to that place searching for suffering and final acts of life,

I see the reactions surrounding my final journey to escape and force the outcome, to force a

closure,

~

the tears are endless from scene to scene, and they are salty and stream like rivers in a dramatic

liquid catastrophe caused by force,

~

I see my garments saturated in every scene by blood,

by sweat from fear and from salty tears leaving visible stains,

~

I hear the wallowing echoing sounds of tragic ballads resonating in the background,

like a funeral chorus the words and the music hasten the pace and give the scenes meaning to

that place,

~

I have the power to stop the ending,

I long for it and drive the events with each poetic word hammering down like nails into soft

wood,

like a punishing crucifixion, the most symbolic willingness to suffer,

~

the crowds gather in that place and there are friends, past and present,

there are relatives, there are lovers too, all gathered for the final ending...

September 2010 – Buenos Aires, Argentina

THE STAND

When life seems to take it's toll,

I will stand by you,

When you've trouble finding your soul,

I will help you through,

~

These tragedies and memories,

that tore our worlds apart,

The burdens and betrayal,

making us not trust our heart,

~

I guess it is all over now,

there's nothing we can do,

Confiding in each other,

it will lead us to what's true,

~

I don't really know,

where our souls will head from here,

but I can make this promise,

I will never disappear,

~

Our lives have suffered many things,

we had to let them go,

There's many things that you've been through,

that I will never know,

~

But I can guarantee you,

that I'll try to understand,

When you think you've lost your way,

I'll lend a helping hand,

~

Standing here together,

in a fragile bleak abyss,

Finding ways to fill the void,

to place our souls in bliss,

~

You are earning my respect

because I consider you a friend,

You seem to have loyalty,

so I'll be there until the end...

December 21, 2015 – Johnston, Rhode Island, USA

A NEW FRIEND, A NEW SOUL, A NEW SONG

I saw her presence in the room,

and wondered how she arrived without a sound,

I noticed her quiet humble elegance,

and how she always seemed to draw a crowd,

~

I wondered who she really was inside,

and why she spawned such curiosity,

I imagined her in a musical sequence,

in my romantic dream walking gracefully,

~

I want to know her soul and to read her mind,

to memorize all of her words and stop the time,

she is statuesque, ever poised and majestic,

yet so real, sublime and full of substance,

~

her words are honest, her feelings intense,

and she reveals a deep soul full of hunger,

I hope I will be her friend and a confidant,

someone she will trust without fear or device,

~

I think I want her friendship in my life...

October 17, 2015 - Johnston, Rhode Island, USA

THE GIRL ON THE STAIRS

I can't help watching you climb those stairs,

and like a lioness you move with grace,

like colors of autumn leaves in your hair,

I wonder in amazement and study your face,

~

who is this living sculpture, a work of art,

what are her thoughts as she climbs,

she blooms like flower gardens in a park,

I just want to know what's on her mind,

~

she doesn't speak and she doesn't seem to smile,

she comes alone and doesn't say anything at all,

I wonder if she could tell me the story of her life,

and I would memorize it and write on my wall,

~

her body speaks a foreign language to me,

her eyes always averted to anyone's gaze,

I think is she Italian, Hispanic or Portuguese,

I'll find the courage to ask in a few more days,

~

she captures me putting me in a trance,

and I can't concentrate on anything else ,

I try not to stare so I just sneak a glance,

for fear she might become afraid of myself,

~

how do I approach this mysterious woman,

who is on the stairs just climbing away?

does she know I composed this silly poem,

as my silent tribute and romantic serenade?

~

will I ever have the courage to speak to her,

to say hi and ask for her musical name?

will she respond in kind and accept my gesture,

or will she abruptly leave and push me away?

~

I'm amazed by this girl on the stairs,

and I can't stop thinking about her,

I am dying to ask her about her hair,

and want to know even more about her,

~

is she in love with someone else,

or is she in between relationships?

is she married or getting divorced?

or is she only looking for friendship?

~

how do I convince her I am for real?

how do I reach her mysterious heart?

my words are true and they reveal,

my hidden feelings from so far apart...

August 16, 2017 - Johnston, Rhode Island, USA

GUILTY OBSSESSIONS

far ever so far away from the world outside,

I retreat into the dark where everything dies,

so alone with depressing thoughts and emotions,

never ending cycles of nightmares and explosions,

~

forcing myself to forget people, names and faces,

resisting anxiety and curiosity's temptations,

when will the memories and regrets finally die?

when will life and time let me walk on by?

~

how much longer will my soul torture my heart?

will I ever heal these insides torn apart?

how many articles and books must I read?

are there any films or videos left to see?

~

I've drowned in heartbreak familiar topic,

and foretells my future like a prophet,

time to abandon weakness and pain,

just wake up and start life over again...

December 02, 2019 – Charlotte, NC & Detroit, MI

CHESTNUT RAINBOWS

my eyes never miss that hair that flows,

moving and changing under the lights...

~

and with some purpose to where she goes,

gracefully, like a bird in flight...

~

those colors woven like soiled yarn,

in so many styles and amber shades...

~

I see the earth beneath her farm,

rows of chestnut trees on parade...

~

senna and brown and golden beige,

cocoa and creme and hazelnut...

~

rich colors that her hair displays,

darkened roots are masked underfoot...

~

twisted threads tangled together,

where fingers and hands run through...

~

strands dictating a silent letter,

how the sunlight changed their hue...

~

mahogany, oak and sandalwood,

yellow streams of grainy lumber...

~

influential giants that once stood,

majestic guardians of leafy treasure...

~

the wind to soften the disappointment,

as she vanishes into her silhouette...

~

so peaceful and yet so unaware,

how she changed my life with her hair...

EPILOGUE

My mother sheltered me very much as a child. I was not street smart or savvy about teen romance, girls and dating. Then along came Shirley who transformed my adolescence in such a short time. She was genuine and loved me with all of her heart and she wanted to run away and start our lives together far away from all of the demons plaguing our little world at that time.

Our lives took many different turns and we never crossed paths at the same time when we could have re-kindled and re-captured our innocent love as kids. We will both forever wonder what life would have been like under different circumstances. We wonder what our children would have looked like and how large our family would have been, etc.

CONCLUSION

After sharing this fist collection of poetry from my past relationships, I believe readers will get a sense of my state of mind. Many times I wrote with tears in my eyes and the saddest music playing in the background. I wrote from pain and suffering. I wrote very early in the morning and many times, very late in the evening. Holidays and weekends passed as I fell asleep with pens and notebooks in front of me, wrinkled and dampened from sweat and tears.

It has become part of me to hide away with my thoughts and emotions, and then record the anguish and pain for posterity. Many years later, I haven't changed and I am still in touch with my inner soul and still feel the impulses and urges. I offer this last poem as a final testament in this first collection. I am sure there will be others soon! Many thanks for enduring till the end!

REMORSEFUL EYES (2016)

pain fills and covers my soul,

all the way down deep inside,

it refuses to ever let me go,

and my inner peace slowly dies,

~

regrets become a daily torture,

and 1001 mistakes are engraved,

all I know is the urge to suffer,

from the hell I seemed to make,

~

how many times can I murder love?

how many more will have to run?

from the self-loathing sorrow,

the guilt im hiding from the sun,

~

the nights are dark and always long,

I live between nightmares and dreams,

and I can hear every single song,

whose lyrics have become my themes,

~

this prison changes colors and sounds,

the people are strangers and friends,

this cycle keeps going round and round,

and there never seems to be an end,

~

I could die a thousand deaths,

worse than any coward born,

and without shame or regret,

no one is called to mourn,

~

for the destroyer of love,

and the murderer of romance,

is condemned from up above,

left never again to dance,

~

guilty of breaking souls,

full of imprisoned emotions,

like an actor playing roles,

a reality coming to fruition,

~

I have lived every life'

other than the one I own'

and traveled a million miles'

and never found my home...

BIBLIOGRAPHY

no external literary sources were consulted for this work

100% original and no references to external publications

AUTHOR BIO

This picture is from 2017, around the time I finished writing the second draft of this manuscript. I know this book is being published in 2022, but I wanted to stay within the mindset of the time frame when I was writing and dealing with the events.

My birth name is Imerio Balletta, and I changed it when I became a US Citizen in 2003. It's a long story, mostly childhood ridicule and bullying.

This is my first published book of petry and I hope I can follow this up with my recent work.

INDEX OF POEMS

Chapter 1 - Julie

Page 11 "What I Saw When We First Met..."

Page 12 "Viendote..." / "Seeing You" (Spanish)

Page 13 "A Cold Winter Night..."

Page 15 "Tormenta Dulce..." / "Sweet Torment" (Spanish)

Page 15 "La Vedevo..." / "I Saw Her" (Italian

Chapter 2 - Stephanie

Page 24 "In One Year..."

Page 24 "On My Knees..."

Page 25 "Love Makes Me Wonder..."

Page 26 "Un Dia, Una Vida, Y Una Poesia..." / "A day, A Life, And A Poem" (Spanish)

Page 27 "A Broken Heart..."

Page 28 "Regrets..."

Page 31 "Hanging Around Life And The Past..."

Page 35 "Hidden Tears..."

Page 76 "Remorseful Eyes..."

Chapter 3 - Ada

Page 43 "Due Goccie D'Acqua..." / "Two Drops Of Water" (Italian)

Page 44 "Mariposa Delicada..." / "Delicate Butterfly" (Spanish)

Page 46 "Nei Giorni Di Te..." / "In The Days Of You" (Italian)

Page 48 "Nero Sul Bianco..." / "Black On White" (Italian)

Page 49 "Labbra Tue..." / "Your Lips" (Italian)

Page 50 "Lei, L'Amore E La Penna..." / "Her, Love, And The Pen" (Italian)

Page 51 "E Poi..." / "And Then..." (Italian)

Page 52 "Sempre Di Piu..." / "Always More" (Italian)

Chapter 4 - Shirley

Page 57 "Two Teens..."

Chapter 5 – Random Poetry

Page 60 "The Storm Is My Soul..."

Page 61 "Summer Wind..."

Page 62 "The Sanctuary..."

Page 63 "French Rain..."

Page 64 "That Place..."

Page 65 "The Stand..."

Page 67 "A New Friend, A New Soul, A New Song... "

Page 68 "The Girl On The Stairs..."

Page 71 "Guilty Obsessions..."

Page 72 "Chestnut Rainbows..."

Made in the USA
Columbia, SC
20 September 2022

67330315R00046